O Suburbia

O Suburbia

by

John Eppel

Published by
Weaver Press, Box A1922, Avondale, Harare. 2018
<www.weaverpresszimbabwe.com>

Earlier versions of some of these poems first appeared in
Kubatana (online), Books Live (online), Avbob (South
Africa), *Stanzas* (South Africa), *Sonata for Matabeleland*
(Snailpress / Baobab Books), *Spoils of War* (Carrefour Press),
The Caruso of Colleen Bawn ('amaBooks),
White Man Crawling ('amaBooks)
They are reproduced here with the kind permission of the
publishers.

Typeset by Weaver Press
Photograph of John Eppel courtesy of Violette Kee Tui
Cover photo by Violette Kee Tui of a painting by Tony
Ronaldson. Art informing art informing art.
Cover Design: Weaver Press Harare.
Printed by: …, Harare.

ISBN: 978-1-77922-345-6 p/b)
ISBN: 978-1-77922-346-3 (e/pub)

John Eppel, 2017

Born in South Africa in 1947, **John Eppel** was raised in Zimbabwe, where he still lives, now retired, in Bulawayo. His first novel, *D G G Berry's The Great North Road*, won the M-Net prize and was listed in the *Weekly Mail & Guardian* as one of the best 20 South African books in English published between 1948 and 1994. His second novel, *Hatchings*, was short-listed for the M-Net prize and was chosen for the series in the *Times Literary Supplement* of the most significant books to have come out of Africa. His other novels are *The Giraffe Man, The Curse of the Ripe Tomato, The Holy Innocents, Absent: The English Teacher, Traffickings,* and (awaiting publication) *The Boy Who Loved Camping*.

Eppel's poetry collections include *Spoils of War*, which won the Ingrid Jonker prize, *Sonata for Matabeleland, Selected Poems: 1965 – 1995, Songs My Country Taught Me,* and *Landlocked: New and Selected Poems from Zimbabwe,* which was a winner in the international Poetry Workshop Prize, Judged by Billy Collins. Furthermore he has collaborated with Philani Amadeus Nyoni in a collection called *Hewn From Rock*, and with Togara Muzanenhamo in a collection called *Textures*, which won the 2015 NOMA Award. He has published three collections of poetry and short stories: *The Caruso of Colleen Bawn, White Man Crawling,* and, in collaboration with the late Julius Chingono, *Together*. His single collection of short stories is entitled *White Man Walking*.

Eppel's short stories and poems have appeared in many anthologies, journals and websites, including six poems in the *Penguin Anthology of South African Poetry*. His poem, 'Vendor and Child' was chosen by *New Internationalist* for their collection, *Fire in the Soul*, the best 100 human rights poems from across the world over the last 100 years. His poem, 'Jasmine' was chosen as 'Poem of the Week' in the *Guardian*.

For Ruth and Tansy

Contents

Pied Crows

The floaters in my damaged eye transform,
grow wings, and soar into the other blue;
catch thermals, ground gymnogenes, ride the storm,
determine what is false and what is true.
Philosophers are crows that mess with me,
upset my garbage, mock my human fears;
disturb with ugly nests, the beefwood tree,
confound the Christmas beetles in my ears.
To croak or not to croak – yes – be my guide
as putrefaction seeps into the light.
Words lie, will lie, words always lied,
but you have substance, fragments of the night.
Now fold your wings, evacuate the sky,
transform to floaters in my damaged eye.

The Clothes Dictators Wear

Cloth creases, even worsted, with old age;
tones, even tyrants', turn cataract blue;
the folded hanky, stained with rheum; the shame

of water marks upon the fly; the rage
of effeminate fists inclined to slew,
limp-wristed, around gatherings of lame

duck eggheads that feed Zimbabwe to gold
diggers, carpetbaggers, corporations
with logos that excite children, excite

mistresses with gross appetites for old
holders of fierce contending nations,
feral dogs dragging promise into night;

dragging suits more wrinkled, more vaguely hung,
no longer moving like a second skin
though once bespoke. But now the lily folds,

the prostate nudges the bladder, the lung
is bunged, the lip minced; and the Botox grin
like pressed cloth, dry-cleaning, coat hangers, holds,

holds an Italian design, choosy, slick:
a three-piece suit on a tottering stick.

Fragments

[A *sestina*]

Possum swopped muses for Moses, Pound said,
whiles *he* forsook them for the living dead:
'active' men like Ulysses, men who led
their people out of the suburbs, who bled,
questing – for what? – the great bass beyond bed-
time stories from Uncle Remus? Ahead,

he cries, ahead! Brer Rabbit had a head
for sculptors; an inclination, it's said,
by you and collaborators, to bed,
like prophets and dictators, the undead
women enthralled by *il poeta* ; bled
hearts for him. Meanwhile Mussolini led

Pound from delight to 'wisdom', disabled
the lyricist, the trickster; plunged him head-
long into the trough of jewsury, bled
all compassion from his veins. Cocteau said,
a rower on the river of the dead
is he. Yes indeedy, It ain't no bed

of roses living with old Ezra the bed-
wetter (ask Olga); the fascist who led
his inmates astray, led them to the dead-
end of the Cantos, from the fountainhead
of petals on a wet … best left unsaid.

Hitler, economics, disenabled

Il miglior fabbro. Possum's fabled
words are tactful rather than true. No bed,
no belt, in the Pisan cage where they said
you would be shot or hanged. You were misled,
turning the pentameter on its head.
Long live the poet; the poet is dead.

At San Michele, island of the dead
where words and song and dance, not bodies, bled
the blood of exiles, you will find a head-
stone marking the American's last bed,
with his ultimate lover who had led
him to silence ten years before, you said.

Yes, that's what you said; it's still in my head –
Beatrice beds in the land of the dead,
where fragments are led, where poems are bled.

Holding Back

'And they made their lives bitter with hard bondage'
[Exodus 1:14]

Late rains hold back the yellowing of soles,
hold back the hardening of devil thorns,
the dates for crickets to address their holes
now devastating our suburban lawns;
hold back those herbs those bitter herbs that keep
worms hesitating like priests between
copse and corpse, open-eyed in troubled sleep,
drying to parchment Blake's echoing green;
herbs to commemorate the Israelites:
scent of camphor, rosemary, taste of gall,
peeping button-like from demolished sites
where the eyes of hungry ghouls appall,
where cats wait patiently for errant moles –
late rains holding back these bellowing souls.

Threnody for My Mother

You determined who got the string
from the rolled roast beef,
the pope's nose, the crispier wing –
O the grief, the grief.

You decided on Christmas day
which crackers to pull,
whose turn it was, not Dad's, to pray -
O my heart is full.

You kissed us better in the night,
kissed for heaven's sake,
crossed the darkness with candle light -
O the ache, the ache.

You healed our pets, you darned our socks,
nurtured every toy,
and now you whisper from the rocks -
O the joy, the joy.

Manifesto

In addition to our dear spouses
and our allocation of small houses,
we will have an escort in every town,
growth-point and village: novice, hand-me-down,
school girl, slut... whatever takes our fancy.
We will relegate to sties all nancy
boys, to kennels all dykes, who will be cured,
in God's good time, well and truly skewered,
by patriotic soldiers with long poles.
Sell-outs will be buried in ant bear holes
after overturning, or hitting trees.
All judges will be given factories
to asset-strip; and generals will get mines,
with free access to anything that shines.
All policemen loyal to the Party
will be allowed to keep their bribes. Hearty
support will be given to servile priests,
and Russians will be entertained with feasts
using cattle from sycophantic whites:
Rhodesians with insatiable appetites
for four-by-fours, biltong, safari camps,
the nostalgic smell of paraffin lamps.
Aliens will be cast into outer
darkness. The First Lady will obtain her
beauty products from Harrods and Dubai.
We will encourage white people to die

because it's only then that we can trust
Blair's kith and kin. "Eternity or Bust"
Is our slogan. We affirm that bullets
are mightier than ballots, and true lies
make a nation healthy, wealthy, and wise.
We will double the strength of the forces,
give them live ammunition and horses
to crush traitors who disturb our cities
(especially girls who bare their titties.)
We will not tolerate freedom of speech,
freedom of assembly, freedom of each
and every citizen to criticize
our Excellency: all knowing; strong ties
with North Korea; Africa's Jesus!
Nations prostrate themselves when he sneezes,
and the world entire is shaken to bits
when Big Boy squats on his people – and shits.

Apartment Blues

[London 1973]

Woke to the smell of breakfast from a dozen kitchens,
dressed as yesterday
and went for the post.
No post. Washed,
ate half a loaf of bread
and regretted it.
Wrote two letters, began a third.
Made tea,
dreamed of success.
Rummaged through the drawers –
no luck.
Stared at a crack in the plaster,
discovered faces.
Heard suddenly the clock.
Sipped tea and sighed a little.

Watched the Saturday afternoon musical on BBC2,
made tea,
scraped burnt milk off the stove,
ate half a loaf of bread
and regretted it.
Watched rain darkening the window ledge,
dreamed.
Went for a walk in the drizzle,
listened to the drains,

saw children playing with a spaniel.
Bought a paper,
ordered tea, and read
that Noel Coward was dead.
Walked back through the drizzle,
climbed into bed, and sighed a little.

Camping at Mtshelele Dam

As night turns purple, with the last bird's call,
and the emerging moon lights up the sky -
antithetical to Lucifer's fall,
who'd been perching too close to God on high -

the stars are amethysts, slow receding,
the love of red and the wisdom of blue;
unseen now, but vernonia feeding
the larvae of lovely-wings: nip and chew;

with foxgloves fibrillating in the breeze
that wafts from the lilied water. And
here's no good and evil, no god to please,
no devil to flatter, here is no grand

Manichaean contest; here's the plop
of barbel in the bankside sedge,
here's a space where time will have a stop,
camping with loved ones at the world's edge.

Femmes Fatale

[after Botticelli]

I use the same knife to amputate my
little toe, and to cut the olive twig
poised like a paint brush; then turn to the sigh
reeking of locust, wild honey, dried fig,
which escapes from your slackening mouth, dear
John. Notice how like a pencil I hold
the dudgeon. Look carefully at the smear
of our blood mingled with slime in a fold
of my lace-edged smock.

                  There's a wind blowing
against us; our water bottles are dry,
and there's some kind of conflict going
on in the background. Many souls will fly.
My slave, bearing your head on hers, looks vexed,
but I'm resigned: your cousin will be next.

Boarding School Life

The entire dorm was madly in love
with the housemaster's cart-wheeling daughter
who whistled 'O for the wings of a dove'
in full spread. We, as lambs to the slaughter,
opened our mouths in a collective gape,
peeping like Toms at Lady Godiva.
Unrequited desire is the inscape
of a boarder. To be a survivor
he must concentrate on mathematics,
on rugby, tackling hard below the knees;
on boxing, cross-country, acrobatics,
the Periodic Table, Socrates…
and if they sprinkle bluestone in his tea,
he'll drop the cartwheels for Geography.

Kiewietjies

Our totem, our familiar, was the crowned
plover that populated the playing
fields of Milton. They made a screeching cry
of alarm when we almost crushed their eggs
or worse, their chicks, in vulnerable nests:
slight scrapes in the ground. In wintry July,
attired incongruously in blazers
and slops, carrying our two shillings worth,
once a week, Thursdays, of tuck shop goodies:
two tickey-cools flavoured orange and green,
six pink marshmallow fish, six apricots,
and a peppermint crisp; *rekkens* round our
necks to pot at pied crows, and a rolled up
exercise book for playing open gates
or touch rugby: we made our way to Top
Field where the flocks were largest, chikkering
away, foraging – run, stop, run, stop, run -
for termites or, after guti, earthworms.

What drove me to it I shall never know,
but I broke its leg with the catapult,
swivelling my aim from a raucous crow...
the First Team rugby posts began to tilt,
the lapwings faded into their own din.

We chased the wounded bird and brought it down.
My friends said I had yielded to a sin –

they touched its leg and stroked its candid crown;
tied it, feebly quarrelling, to my chest.
I have to keep it there until it dies.
My adolescent heart became its nest.
It's with me still. Kiewiet, kiewiet, it cries.

A Brief Address to the Ghost of Percy Bysshe Shelley

Where you raised a small turf altar
to the mountain-walking Pan,
my goddess's footsteps falter
over paper thorns. The man

whose bed she warmed, a dying
Jew, King David was his rank,
so young then, so lovely, lying
naked by that withered flank.

Now she lies with me, not in my bed,
the girl from Shunem, still coy,
lying on thorns inside my head;
in your words, an unbodied joy,

in mine a longing of the flesh
while words, like paper thorns, enmesh.

Mise-en-Abyme

When actors
act Hamlet,
they are acting
an actor
who acts himself
as an actor
of actors.

The Magnificent Seven

Seven finches in a row
guard the fledglings down below.
Monday looks at life askance,
Tuesday's got a narrow glance;
Wednesday checks the sky for hawks,
Thursday notes the cat that stalks;
Friday seems about to fly,
Saturday gives me the eye;
Sunday seems the most at ease,
not too fazed by what it sees.
Seven finches in a row
guarding fledglings down below.

Waxbill

Like my safari-suit, same powder blue;
like the plumbago (Cecil's favourite
flower) that hedges me in; like the few
remaining stills of my father's eyes; bit
by bit, little by little, hippity-
hopping from place to place; pecking at shame,
at stubble, at grains of time; frequently
splashing your chums in the bath; far too tame
for your own good (my cat is on a quest);
like Bulawayo skies… you absorb me.
My home sits also near a hornets' nest:
will they impound it? Will they let me be?
Underneath the thorns, you pick and you choose;
your tremolo gets me singing the blues.

Those About to Play

Celebrities are the gladiators
of neoliberalism.
they don't fight fires,
they don't fight floods,
they don't fight disease,
they fight each other.

They fight each other
in coliseums
like Hollywood,
the Super Bowl,
Madison Square Gardens,
Cable News Network.

The Masters of the universe
use them to distract
the poor in spirit,
the meek,
the merciful,
the peacemakers.

Ave, Imperator,
qui ad ludere,
te salutant.

Those Dark Acacias

[circa 1968]

...and I feel the music throbbing
through those dark acacia trees,
hectic palpitations pitching
pods in a game with the breeze,
and the drone of beetles darting
round like model aeroplanes.

I am sitting on the granite wall
above the laughing drains
that gurgle round and down among
our village public ways,
and you are with the music,
and the others, and their praise.

And when you take the high road home
with moonlight in your eye,
someone's jacket round your shoulders,
someone's fingers on your thigh -
when you pass those dark acacias
you may hear the branches sigh.

They are sighing after music
that has had a 'dying fall'
in the laughter of hyenas,
in the nightjar's creaking call,
in a Sunday evening sickness
stretched along the granite wall.

My Father's Tool Box

This is the story that the Sandman tells:
It started as an ammunition box,
a wooden crate packed with howitzer shells -
part of a plan to rout the Desert Fox.

Your father found it empty, discarded,
hard by the railhead at Mersa Matruh.
Intact, though with a slightly damaged lid,
it kept his puttees from the foggy dew.

After the war he brought the plunder home,
repaired the lid, renewed the rope handles,
painted it red and packed it with cheap, chrome-
plated tools, grease, spare matches and candles.

When fate came calling, he left it to you,
you emptied it (that smell of oil, that hint
of cordite), scraped it and painted it blue,
filled it with cuddly toys and peppermint,

filled it with dressing-up clothes, porcelain
dolls, the little red hen, the gingerbread
man; filled it with soldiers made out of tin...
Sandman is back in the realm of the dead.

End of an Affair

The alarm clock shot me awake
to an applause of rain
drops. I fell out of bed bowing,
and then you poured in like
a mug of steaming chocolate.

I climbed back into bed, snuggled
against the cooling sheets
and dreamt of getting dressed, until
it was too late for break-
fast and a proper wash. My love.

An Awakening

She stretches, slowly, like a time-lapsed tulip
opening to the light, like the effect
of codeine on a throbbing head; lets slip
a silver bangle, which rolls, slowly, checked
by friction on the floor and in the air;
viscosity; slow… slower… shuddering
to a stopped condition; like aftercare
when loving goes wrong, or droplets that cling
to leaves after rain, to old garden taps…
slowly succumbing… stretching… changing shape;
she yawns without covering her mouth, slaps
an imagined mosquito, rubs the nape
of her neck; slowly, sweetly, turns to me
and says she's ready for a cup of tea.

With a Sore Knee

Full of shadows
and silence
is the nature
reserve as
it spreads like thighs
to let me
through on my bike
bearing too
much weight for the
back wheel: I
couldn't leave my
poems be-
hind as well as
my OUCH friends.

I Know Now where the People Go

[January 1967]

I know now where the people go, that is, when people die:
I often see their faces in the clouds above the sky;
and in the trees at twilight time when silhouette is bold,
the branches and the leaves, to me, are faces thousand fold.
And if, by chance, there is a breeze, clouds drift and
      branches leap,
some faces tip a wink at me, some coyly take a peep.

Fathers' Day

I went to shut the gate;
the dogs were waiting
anxiously; I was late;
I'd been listening

to the McCormack tape:
'The Rose of Tralee'.
It helps me to escape
actuality:

the work – you know – the guilt;
also being male
and white, and having spilt
things. 'Yes, my tail-

thumping companions, I
see you,' your insane,
full-moon faces, sky-
turned, not expecting rain.

A cool wind blows, making
the dry air drier.
Your lucky bean is raking
the sand for moisture.

I bet it rains a lot

in Tralee. 'The pale
moon was rising…' it's not
pale here; it's a hale

and hearty, sun-tanned god
of mongrels and late,
a last, late goldenrod.
We sprint for the gate.

You Ask Me Why

Tall trees with elbows stretch against the sky
to tickle breezes as they bicker by,
and catch the sunlight's gaudy yellow glare
with leaves as bright as polished silverware.
The grass is long and thick and golden green
with crowds of peeping cosmos in-between
the wiry tufts and blades. But on the ground
are plastic bags and beer cans littered round
like ID photos at the Lost and Found.
And that is why I push my glasses off and turn away
before I lose that light, that glimmer, of a lovely day.

Seeking Identity

I look for my self
in family, friends,
home and garden,
grass, flowers, rocks, trees…

all the while resisting
my gender,
my skin colour,
my nationality.

Artificial Intelligence

[June, 1968]

A robot is a hairless man with different coloured eyes
and everybody knows that he is infinitely wise.
I saw a woman selling stamps behind four brassy bars,
and on the kerb a hairless man commanding motor cars.
I saw a bank clerk lick his pen then test it on a sheet,
and on the flags three-coloured eyes, controller of the street.
He blinks an eye and people stop, or move, or hesitate,
respect the pressure of his look – Take care! Now go! Now
    wait!
He needs no speech to shout commands nor arms to wave
    about,
he leaves it to humanity to paw the air and shout.
But in the end, man's better off, as far as I can see,
for, to a dog three-coloured eyes is just another tree.

September

Nature is an impressionist in my
part of town, especially now when light
choked with dust and pollen and garbage smoke
permeates cry after cry of lost bush
birds. Vesper bats stroke the palpitating
moon about to run is yolk, while crickets,
rain frogs, tune up for the Bulawayo
proms. It's all sepia, *mielie* stalks, burnt
orange, sienna… restless is the word,
September restlessness; New Year babies
pushed from Virgo's partial thighs; starry thighs,
purpler than priests, than stains of inky wine.
Starry, starry impressionistic light
hesitating on the doorstep of night.

Kunstwollen

My will-to-form, my verbal arabesques
conceived on mountain tops, in beds, at desks;
asleep, awake, on buses drifting south,
along the Matseumhlope to its mouth:
a vent that swallows and regurgitates,
rolls off the tongue, trippingly, masticates
the news, the party line. My *fleur-de-lis*,
my conical tower, my sisters three,
muses, curlicues of traveller's joy,
spandrels that excite the wondering boy;
wandering west, its window like a rose,
bells on her fingers and rings on her toes.
I hesitate northwards, veer to the east -
my wreaths, my palmettes – my moveable feast.

Drinking Tea

The matron sighed and drained her second cup:
'Yes, dear,' she said, 'my time is almost up.
I'm growing old, you know – damn nearly sixty-eight;
Saint Peter's waiting for me at the gate.

'Sometimes at night when youth is sound asleep,
old people turn the pages of their lives and weep
for what has gone and what will never be…
I think I'll have another cup of tea.'

The Poet

She lives closer to the moon,
her hair up one day, down the next,
eats peanut butter from a spoon,
is often and seldom perplexed.

She takes her time in the loo,
most comfortable chair of all,
working on a clerihew,
dressed only in her grandma's shawl.

'Mary Shelley,
I turn to jelly
when I read your story:
so grim and gory.'

She loves tortoises and guinea pigs,
her ankles are thicker than thin;
she blows the insects from wild figs
and claims there's no such thing as sin.

Closer to the moon she lives,
perching in the branches of trees;
whenever she takes, she gives, gives,
holding back, then breaking, a sneeze.

I love her for her quirky ways
too late for some, for some too soon,
Like when she farts 'La Marseillaise' -
O daughter of the dipping moon.

Haiku

About red and white
tablecloths, there is something
so reassuring.

Geography Lesson

Yesterday I dreamed the hours
in teeming fields of summer flowers,
inhaling skies of drowsy air
while insects scuttled everywhere.
There was such life beneath the grass
that I, for one, would sooner pass
an afternoon in wonder there
than dull at desk, with bum on chair.

Today at desk, with bum on chair
I turn a page and pull my hair
and turn a page and force my brain
to focus on the 'coastal plain'.
Then, all too soon, attention yields,
and I am sprawling in the fields.

Doves

You are the least symbolical of birds;
never mind that you brought the olive twig
back to Noah, that you represented
the Holy Spirit, and faithful marriage.
You are randy, aggressive, tough; not nerds
like budgies and song finches. You doves jig
on the road; I've seen you; watched you outbid
crows for carrion, escort the carriage
of lust, along with grim-eyed lions, bears,
fleet leopards, ravenous for deer. What's this
about spotless white feathers … world peace?

O Columbia, you've had a bum rap;
false charges all. Allow me to release
you into my garden where you belong,
and teach me the words of Solomon's song.

Tumbling

The stars, I think, are tumbling from my eye,
that grain of corn, the moon, a shibboleth,
which helps my enemies identify
a rhymester with his smoking-candle breath.
My name is whispered in the dead of night:
a woman's voice awakes me from my dreams;
they tumble back, the stars, they give me light
to check the time, to re-connect, to… "'Seems,'
madam! Nay, it is; I know not 'seems'". (John!)
A voice I recognise not-quite, calling
me; a woman's voice, from where? – on and on
like starlight freezing into clicks; falling,
galling. Is that voice breathing in my head,
(John?) tumbling from the living or the dead?

Five Five-Line Stanzas

And they're all men
these prophets
with their three-piece suits,
dark glasses,
Italian-styled shoes;

and they persuade you,
yes you!
to drink their urine,
lick their sweat,
breathe insecticide.

Why? Why do you do it?
You *nouveau riche*
who already have enough money,
thanks to your connections,
to go on shopping sprees

to Dubai, Singapore, Johannesburg,
occasionally even to Harrods.
Orgasmic moaning when he speaks to God
on his smart phone,
when he puts his devil in your hell.

How easy then is it
for our politicians
to convince you
that they are in it
not for themselves but for you?

One for the Road

Shedding its skin like a serpent, the moon,
approaching its fifteenth night, rolls along
the Great North Road, past West Nicholson, past

the Jessie Hotel, dusting the bushveld
with pollen, slowing down at Colleen Bawn,
picking up, near Gwanda, the last balloon

of the last party, now bobbing, about
to pop, past Bala Bala, Essexvale…
BANG… it flivvers into Bulawayo.

Stillness

I am attached to stillness,
the stillness of rocks and trees
and endless April evenings
unstirred by brook or breeze;

of moonlight on these withered hands
that once bent six-inch nails;
once held in trust a brown-eyed girl.
Now reason, impulse countervails.

I am attached to stillness,
the stillness of roosting birds,
of memories that float like dust,
and poems without words.

In Praise of Granite

[after W.H. Auden]

That essence of human middens, tissues
tinct with yellow and brown like autumn leaves,
Kleenex chiefly, is the stone. What issues
from its cracks, what crumbles, to-heaven heaves,
heaping stone on stone, glinting mica, all
along Maleme valley, offering
nothing and everything. When boulders fall
from celestial heights, or rise, exploding,
from the baleful depths, don't, do not, delay
or hasten that ride. When the skeleton
with a cock calls, hornblende high, quartz-pocked clay
stiffening, feldspar nudging the scats, grin
back, embrace the cloaked ribs, straddle the bone,
let urine, coursing lichen, set in stone.

Words

Language is fungal
words live and die like mushrooms
some are poisonous

Snapshot

We're swinging on a Firestone tyre,
my brother, my sister, and me;
its arc takes in maDube's *khaya*
and the *ichithamuzi* tree.

My sister's wearing polka dots,
my brother's wearing shoes,
and I am wearing forget-me-nots
in pinks and whites and blues.

It swings us high, it swings us low,
the Firestone company;
it swings us where the folks don't go:
Bobby, Patty, and me.

After a Heat Wave

In shot silk slippers
rain tippy-toes upon my
roof. Deliverance.

A Settler's Taunt

You can deny me
my birth status but
you cannot deny
me my death status:
death will fix me in
the soil forever.

ICU: Mater Dei, Bulawayo

No, don't try to sit up:
all those tubes,
those poor speechless mouths,
the unshaven look (not your style),
complexion of a winding-sheet,
skeleton with a *boep*.
Don't try to recognise me;
don't be embarrassed by my hand on yours;
go back to your ramblings
on the playing fields of yesteryear;
go back to the day we beat New Zealand,
to convoy duty on the Plumtree road,
to Christmas Pass, Christmas Day, 1890.
Go further back, my friend,
to Gulubahwe Cave
on the Old Gwanda Road
where the turtle that swims in the rock
will guide you to your next life.

Dying Poet

She sewed a band of silk into his hat,
his travelling hat. Woodhouse took a lock
of hair. The poet coughed, looked, and said, 'That
drop of blood is my death warrant'. The shock
shook tremors: Severn whimpered, Brown turned pale,
in her diary Fanny wrote, 'Mr Keats
leaves Hampstead', and soon the pair set sail
for Rome, the Spanish Steps, the bustling streets,
the bed of death. 'It will be easy', he
consoled his friend, whose breathing pressed like ice
upon his wasted lungs. A cemetery
where fast fading violets bloom should suffice.
Letters lay unopened, days grew shorter
for him whose name would be writ in water.

The Dog-meat Vendor

Salutations to the dog-meat vendor,
he skins and guts the ones put down by vets;
his cuts, half rotten, are sweet and tender.

He sets no store by breed or gender,
He traps no strays, he abducts no pets;
salutations to the dog-meat vendor.

Neither a borrower nor a lender,
not too worried about whom he upsets;
his cuts, half rotten, are sweet and tender.

The one at the helm, the great pretender,
has plunged his people into untold debts;
salutations to the dog-meat vendor.

No one places blame on this offender;
starving citizens must have no regrets.
his cuts, half rotten, are sweet and tender.

This villanelle has just one agenda:
appreciate what poverty begets.
His cuts, half rotten, are sweet and tender.
Salutations to the dog-meat vendor.

Teaching 'King Lear'

I told my students:
after the first reading
you will giggle;
after the second reading
you will be silent;
after the third reading
you will weep.

Wind Behaving Badly

The clouds descend, the firmament grows grey,
a churning wind, bone-cold, assaults the trees,
blowing petals and little girls away
before relaxing to a shirtless breeze.
Again it rises flapping doeks and scarves,
banging casements, matrons, widows, wives...
whistling through cracks, keyholes, while it carves
that look in daddy's eyes. Run for your lives.
The clouds ascend, the firmament blows blue,
the rising wind lifts skirts and lashes hair –
what's true is false, my child, what's false is true –
the white sheets shaking, raking underwear.
Behaving-badly-winds will not subside
till you, my dears, commit tyrannicide.

In the Matobo Hills

We have the world to ourselves,
waiting for the moment
when the setting sun meets the rising moon.
Their size is equal;
their radiance is equal.
The light of consciousness merges
with the darkness of instinct.

We sip our wine on the threshold
of time and eternity.
We are neither male nor female:
we are perfection.
Like salt dolls, in the words of Ramakrishna,
like salt dolls walking into the ocean,
we lose ourselves together with the world.

Fingering

[after *The Guitar Lesson* by Balthus]

Abandoned on the floor a child's guitar,
abandoned on the teacher's lap, a child.
The teacher's gaze is near, the girl's far, far
from the yellow ribbon, the slippers mild,
the stockings downrolled from her parted knees,
the dress thrown back from her belly button;
the teacher's fingers urging ecstasies
on the fret of her skinny thigh. Glut on,
glut on, you viewers, gazes lingering.
Her pointed breast's exposed, but not to feed;
the temple where she yanks the child will bleed,
is bleeding, down the lifeless arm. A string
snaps, but the poet goes on fingering.

'Nothing Will Come of Nothing'

[King Lear]

It's not quite above the horizon, not
quite below. That it arcs is beyond doubt:
a luminous cable-point, pushing out
of a circle, a shorting of stars, hot
with hours, burning rubber; two carbon
poles separated by a small air space,
all of space, all of time; soft carapace
breaking into two, arcing into one.

Beneath, says Lear, is all the fiend's: "There's hell,
there's darkness… burning, scalding, stench";
his gods won't venture below the girdle;
but that old fool was either in the court
or on the heath; no arc; clench, unclench, clench,
unclench. Naught is nothing and nothing naught.

Daddy Longlegs

A wire hair clip dangling from a wisp
of time, sticky, like similes and words
that rhyme. Skedaddling, an animated
cartoon, from cellar to ceiling, midnight
to noon. Prickling reminders of the old
places and, veiled in cobwebs, the older
faces. You like nothing better than an
empty cardboard box. Always on your toes,
tiny tiddly bits, a mouthful of eggs,
navigating corners, wainscots, in fits
and starts. 8H legs and, boy, can you shake!
You scared Miss Muffet out of her wits
spinning her a shroud. How long will it take?

A Bird of Ill-Omen

A binga banga bongo
It's a cheeky fork-tailed drongo
and he's up against my shoulder
on a binga banga boulder
singing: Somabula coo coo,
snatch a worm from Mrs Hoopoe,
set the finches all afire
with your deep and dark desire.

Well, it's a binga banga bongo
with the cheeky fork-tailed drongo
and he's up against my bladder
and there's nothing makes me madder
singing Matabele bye bye,
nick poor Mrs Nightjar's firefly,
peck the birthday candles out,
promulgate the coming rout.

Crunch Time

Chongololos underfoot,
tiny anthills on the lawn,
stubbled fields,
carrots rinsed at the garden tap,
rusks without coffee -

waiting for results.

Pigs in the orchard,
hyenas at the skinning place,
liquidity,
skulls of protesters,
boots on the ground -

waiting for results.

Love Your Fate

Faith without doubt leads to sanctimony,
sanctimony leads to self-righteousness.
Eli, Eli, lama sabachthani.

Live beyond your time alive, plant a tree;
linger on that crossing to the abyss.
Eli, Eli, lama sabachthani.

Like Nietzsche, love your fate: *amor fati*;
a solitude of shedding leaves is bliss.
Faith without doubt leads to sanctimony.

The word, that word, begun from Galilee
may be a blessing and may be a curse.
Eli, Eli, lama sabachthani.

Love the polished jade of chincherinchee,
the day departing with a fleeting kiss;
faith without doubt leads to sanctimony.

Amor fati, agree to disagree;
be generous, take money from your purse;
faith without doubt leads to sanctimony.
Eli, Eli, lama sabachthani.

Tracks I Remember

Paths with banks of tick-heavy grass tilting
to caress the thigh; roads where dipping
hornbills lead the way, mopani scrub on
either side; tok-tokkies doing headstands,
their fused wings harder than fingernails, tap-
tapping messages of love; antlion
larvae (doodlebugs) crafting pits of death
where the critical angle of repose
slides crawling insects to their doom;
stink of formic acid, of resin, of
crushed locusts, wings in threatening display.

Paths with trip-wires working an explosion;
banks of whispering gun-muzzles, safety
catches clicking like beetles; roads going
nowhere, primed; the relative safety of
middle *mannetjies* where devil thorns cling
to combat boots; farm gates, not quite open,
not quite shut, availing detonators;
cadres, exposed like anthills, keeping still,
stiller than puff adders basking, spiders
playing dead; stink of fear, of corpses
with hand grenades in threatening display.

We Live in Language

We live in language, 'deed we do;
we state that it's a lovely day;
'bout 'this' and 'that' there's much ado.

We want to know what's false, what's true;
we question: will it go away?
We live in language, 'deed we do.

We wonder how, and when, and who,
command, like Knut, the waves to stay;
'bout this and that there's much ado.

And as, like debt, the words accrue,
our exclamations ricochet.
We live in language, 'deed we do.

We think it's two, not to, nor too;
we yearn for loveliness, we pray.
'Bout this and that there's much ado.

Language – what a hullabaloo!
What ashes! What a bright bouquet!
We live in language, 'deed we do;
'bout this-'n-that there's much ado;

Brats

They wear dark glasses that make a statement;
their white denims are even more distressed
than the old folk at Edith Duly Home.
Those high-top sneakers, ideal for clubbing,
for trashing, for swigging, from the bottle,
Moet & Chandon Dom Perignon White Gold,
while their elders back home queue for putrid
dog meat, road-kill, discarded cabbage leaves.

On social media they brag, faces
already beginning to twist and bloat,
bragging to their thousands of admirers
that they are immune from prosecution,
like their progenitors, above the law.
These our sons! They post a flame emoji,
the evening is lit, the government
aides are hovering. You and I will pay.

Let's Drink to Growing Old

I lean against the monkey thorn
planted years ago,
before our youngest child was born,
before the wilting of the corn,
I watched the sapling grow.

I took the seed from Hillside Dams,
soaked it overnight,
before the slaughter of the lambs,
before those drunken dithyrambs,
its bark turned flaky white.

Its hooks are hard and shiny black,
its catkins yellow-gold;
its roughness presses at my back,
each ridge I feel, each scab, each crack,
so, cheers to growing old!

Hadeda. Perched. Misty Conditions.

I see your prospector's pick of a bill
has branched. No place for the iridescence
of your shoulder pads in these neutral tones,
this subfusc. Only the Shona-sculpture
brownish-grey, the hoary moustache, perhaps
the touch of red. Below, your comrades probe
suburbia for worms, snails, Parktown prawns,
and windfall avocado pears. Why won't
you join them? It must be your turn to watch
for errant boys with pellet guns, irate
dads trying to catch the commentator's
voice that you obliterate with your song:
a *vuvuzela* in a spangled tree.

The Gathering

The dead are gathering, even Oupa
with his skinny legs and slickly waving hair,
straight from the Kimberley diamond diggings;
and tight-lipped Ouma, no longer Scottish,
whistling 'Stranger on the shore'; Aunty Nola
in a straw hat that could have floated me
across Kariba; and in his Fairlane,
Uncle Bob, spaced out of his masonic
mind, refusing to remember Tobruk;
our father tramping down the quarry in
his boots, reluctant to acknowledge genes
that carbonate his children's blood. The dead

are gathering, even Mrs Beadon
with her pink blancmange the night before we
took the train to boarding school; our mother,
knitting kaleidoscopic pullovers;
Grandfather Hannan, paying me sixpence
to scratch his wart; even pets, for goodness'
sake: there's Louis chewing through another
safety belt; and Granny Trot, hovering
above the family grave in Lydenburg
saying, 'What a dear little paw paw!
Basil's gone to shoot the crows!' Yes, the dead
are gathering, gathering in my dreams.

Considering Heidegger

The future's not-yet,
the past is no-longer:
in the present you get
stronger and stronger.

Obnubilation

I say, what's happening to our nation
as clouds, like camouflage, obscure the sky,
is nothing short of obnubilation.
Six died, and more, much more than six will die.

I say, what's happening to Zimbabwe
as perspex shields reflecting someone's fear,
tapped by batons outside Hotel Bronte,
with gas and water cannon in the rear,

are by an indistinct transparency
a sign of what has been, what is, will be.

Soft as Wool

But knit that wool into a scarf
in colours of your country's flag,
long, like the neck of a giraffe,
thick, like quality carpet shag;

more stubborn than a hangman's rope,
more cruel than piano wire,
more frightening than a lycanthrope,
more tempting than a sick desire;

then wear it on the hottest days
to hear the people sing your praise.

Glossary of local terms

Kiewietjies: Crowned plovers (Afrikaans)
Tickey cools: sealed plastic tubes of flavoured water
Rekkens: catapults (Afrikaans)
Guti: light drizzle
Lucky bean: coral tree, Erythrina Lysistemon
Robot: traffic lights
Matseumhlope: white stones. A seasonal river that runs
    through Bulawayo (iSindebele)
Maleme: A river in the Matobo hills (iSindebele?)
Khaya: home (iSindebele)
Ichithamusi tree: Apple-leaf, Lonchocarpus capassa
    (iSindebele)
Boep: paunch (Afrikaans)
Doeks: headscarves (Afrikaans)
Chongololos: millipedes
Mopane: Colophospermum mopane (iSindebele)
Tok tokkies   dung beetles (Afrikaans)
Middle-manneties   grass ridge in the middle of a dirt road
    (Afrikaans)
Oupa: grandfather (Afrikaans)
Ouma: grandmother (Afrikaans)
8H   8H leads produce fine lines

Printed in the United States
By Bookmasters